Premier League Football Fixtures

2022/23

By Utopia Press

Match Week 1: 5/8/22

Venue : Selhurst Park

Crystal Palace   vs   Arsenal

Venue : Craven Cottage

Fulham   vs   Liverpool

Venue : Vitality Stadium

Bournemouth   vs   Aston Villa

Venue : St. James' Park

Newcastle   vs   Notts Forest

Venue : King Power Stadium

Leicester City   vs   Brentford

Match Week 1: 5/8/22

Venue : Tottenham Hotspur Stadium

Tottenham   vs   Southampton

Venue : Elland Road

Leeds United   vs   Wolves

Venue : Goodison Park

Everton   vs   Chelsea

Venue : Old Trafford

Man United   vs   Brighton

Venue : London Stadium

West Ham   vs   Man City

Match Week 2: 13/8/22

Venue : Stamford Bridge

Chelsea   vs   Tottenham

Venue : St Mary's Stadium

Southampton   vs   Leeds United

Venue: Emirates Stadium

Arsenal   vs   Leicester City

Venue : Brentford Community Stadium

Brentford   vs   Man United

Venue : Anfield

Liverpool   vs   Crystal Palace

Venue : Villa Park

Aston Villa   vs   Everton

Venue : The City Ground

Notts Forest   vs   West Ham

Venue : Amex Stadium

Brighton   vs   Newcastle

Venue : Etihad Stadium

Man City   vs   Bournemouth

Venue : Molineux Stadium

Wolves   vs   Fulham

Match Week 3: 20/8/22

Venue : Goodison Park

Everton   vs   Notts Forest

Venue : King Power Stadium

Leicester City   vs   Southampton

Venue : Etihad Stadium

West Ham   vs   Brighton

Venue : Craven Cottage

Fulham   vs   Brentford

Venue : Old Trafford

Man United   vs   Liverpool

Match Week 3: 20/8/22

Venue : Tottenham Hotspur Stadium

Tottenham vs **Wolves**

Venue : St. James' Park

Newcastle vs **Man City**

Venue : Elland Road

Leeds United vs **Chelsea**

Venue : Selhurst Park

Crystal Palace vs **Aston Villa**

Venue : Vitality Stadium

Bournemouth vs **Arsenal**

Match Week 4: 27/8/22

Venue : Stamford Bridge

Chelsea   vs   Leicester City

Venue : Molineux Stadium

Wolves   vs   Newcastle

Venue : Villa Park

Aston Villa   vs   West Ham

Venue : St Mary's Stadium

Southampton   vs   Man United

Venue : Amex Stadium

Brighton   vs   Leeds United

Match Week 4: 27/8/22

Venue : The City Ground

Notts Forest   vs   Tottenham

Venue : Etihad Stadium

Man City   vs   Crystal Palace

Venue: Emirates Stadium

Arsenal   vs   Fulham

Venue : Anfield

Liverpool   vs   Bournemouth

Venue : Brentford Community Stadium

Brentford   vs   Everton

Match Week 5: 30/8/22

Venue : Elland Road

Leeds United   vs   Everton

Venue : King Power Stadium

Leicester City   vs   Man United

Venue : Vitality Stadium

Bournemouth   vs   Wolves

Venue : London Stadium

West Ham   vs   Tottenham

Venue : Craven Cottage

Fulham   vs   Brighton

Match Week 5: 30/8/22

Venue: Emirates Stadium

Arsenal   vs   Aston Villa

Venue : Selhurst Park

Crystal Palace   vs   Brentford

Venue : St Mary's Stadium

Southampton   vs   Chelsea

Venue : Anfield

Liverpool   vs   Newcastle

Venue : Etihad Stadium

Man City   vs   Notts Forest

Match Week 6: 3/9/22

Venue : Tottenham Hotspur Stadium

Tottenham   vs   Fulham

Venue : Amex Stadium

Brighton   vs   Leicester City

Venue : Goodison Park

Everton   vs   Liverpool

Venue : Villa Park

Aston Villa   vs   Man City

Venue : The City Ground

Notts Forest   vs   Bournemouth

Match Week 6: 3/9/22

Venue : Stamford Bridge

Chelsea   vs   West Ham

Venue : Brentford Community Stadium

Brentford   vs   Leeds United

Venue : Molineux Stadium

Wolves   vs   Southampton

Venue : St. James' Park

Newcastle   vs   Crystal Palace

Venue : Old Trafford

Man United   vs   Arsenal

Match Week 7: 10/9/22

Venue: Emirates Stadium

Arsenal   vs   Everton

Venue : Elland Road

Leeds United   vs   Notts Forest

Venue : Craven Cottage

Fulham   vs   Chelsea

Venue : Vitality Stadium

Bournemouth vs   Brighton

Venue : St Mary's Stadium

Southampton vs   Brentford

Match Week 7: 10/9/22

Venue : London Stadium

West Ham   vs   Newcastle

Venue : Anfield

Liverpool   vs   Wolves

Venue : Selhurst Park

Crystal Palace   vs   Man United

Venue : King Power Stadium

Leicester City   vs   Aston Villa

Venue : Etihad Stadium

Man City   vs   Tottenham

Match Week 8: 17/9/22

Venue : Stamford Bridge

Chelsea   vs   Liverpool

Venue : Brentford Community Stadium

Brentford   vs   Arsenal

Venue : Molineux Stadium

Wolves   vs   Man City

Venue : Old Trafford

Man United   vs   Leeds United

Venue : Tottenham Hotspur Stadium

Tottenham   vs   Leicester City

Match Week 8: 17/9/22

Venue : Goodison Park

Everton   vs   **West Ham**

Venue : Villa Park

Aston Villa   vs   **Southampton**

Venue : The City Ground

Notts Forest   vs   **Fulham**

Venue : Amex Stadium

Brighton   vs   **Crystal Palace**

Venue : St. James' Park

Newcastle   vs   **Bournemouth**

Venue : Anfield

Liverpool   vs   Brighton

Venue : Craven Cottage

Fulham   vs   Newcastle

Venue : St Mary's Stadium

Southampton   vs   Everton

Venue : King Power Stadium

Leicester City   vs   Notts Forest

Venue: Emirates Stadium

Arsenal   vs   Tottenham

Match Week 9: 1/10/22

Venue : Elland Road

Leeds United   vs   Aston Villa

Venue : Selhurst Park

Crystal Palace   vs   Chelsea

Venue : Vitality Stadium

Bournemouth   vs   Brentford

Venue : London Stadium

West Ham   vs   Wolves

Venue : Etihad Stadium

Man City   vs   Man United

Match Week 10: 8/10/22

Venue : Goodison Park

Everton   vs   Man United

Venue : London Stadium

West Ham   vs   Fulham

Venue : St. James' Park

Newcastle   vs   Brentford

Venue : Vitality Stadium

Bournemouth vs Leicester City

Venue : The City Ground

Notts Forest   vs   Aston Villa

Match Week 10: 8/10/22

Venue : Etihad Stadium

Man City   vs   Southampton

Venue : Stamford Bridge

Chelsea   vs   Wolves

Venue : Amex Stadium

Brighton   vs   Tottenham

Venue: Emirates Stadium

Arsenal   vs   Liverpool

Venue : Selhurst Park

Crystal Palace vs Leeds United

Venue : St Mary's Stadium

Southampton   vs   West Ham

Venue : Anfield

Liverpool   vs   Man City

Venue : Tottenham Hotspur Stadium

Tottenham   vs   Everton

Venue : Molineux Stadium

Wolves   vs   Notts Forest

Venue : Brentford Community Stadium

Brentford   vs   Brighton

Match Week 11: 15/10/22

Venue : King Power Stadium

Leicester City   vs   Crystal Palace

Venue : Old Trafford

Man United   vs   Newcastle

Venue : Elland Road

Leeds United   vs   Arsenal

Venue : Villa Park

Aston Villa   vs   Chelsea

Venue : Craven Cottage

Fulham   vs Bournemouth

Match Week 12: 18/10/22

Venue : Vitality Stadium

Bournemouth vs Southampton

Venue : Amex Stadium

Brighton   vs   Notts Forest

Venue: Emirates Stadium

Arsenal   vs   Man City

Venue : Brentford Community Stadium

Brentford   vs   Chelsea

Venue : King Power Stadium

Leicester City vs Leeds United

Match Week 12: 18/10/22

Venue : Craven Cottage

Fulham   vs   Aston Villa

Venue : Selhurst Park

Crystal Palace vs   Wolves

Venue : St. James' Park

Newcastle   vs   Everton

Venue : Old Trafford

Man United   vs   Tottenham

Venue : Anfield

Liverpool   vs   West Ham

Venue : Molineux Stadium

Wolves   vs   Leicester City

Venue : Villa Park

Aston Villa   vs   Brentford

Venue : Tottenham Hotspur Stadium

Tottenham   vs   Newcastle

Venue : London Stadium

West Ham   vs   Bournemouth

Venue : St Mary's Stadium

Southampton vs   Arsenal

Match Week 13: 22/10/22

Venue : Elland Road

Leeds United   vs   Fulham

Venue : Goodison Park

Everton   vs   Crystal Palace

Venue : Etihad Stadium

Man City   vs   Brighton

Venue : The City Ground

Notts Forest   vs   Liverpool

Venue : Stamford Bridge

Chelsea   vs   Man United

Match Week 14: 29/10/22

Venue : St. James' Park

Newcastle   vs   Aston Villa

Venue : Vitality Stadium

Bournemouth   vs   Tottenham

Venue : Amex Stadium

Brighton   vs   Chelsea

Venue : King Power Stadium

Leicester City   vs   Man City

Venue : Old Trafford

Man United   vs   West Ham

Match Week 14: 29/10/22

Venue: Emirates Stadium

Arsenal   vs   Notts Forest

Venue : Selhurst Park

Crystal Palace   vs   Southampton

Venue : Anfield

Liverpool   vs   Leeds United

Venue : Brentford Community Stadium

Brentford   vs   Wolves

Venue : Craven Cottage

Fulham   vs   Everton

Match Week 15: 5/11/22

Venue : Stamford Bridge

Chelsea vs **Arsenal**

Venue : The City Ground

Notts Forest vs **Brentford**

Venue : Villa Park

Aston Villa vs **Man United**

Venue : Tottenham Hotspur Stadium

Tottenham vs **Liverpool**

Venue : St Mary's Stadium

Southampton vs **Newcastle**

Match Week 15: 5/11/22

Venue : Molineux Stadium

Wolves   vs   Brighton

Venue : London Stadium

West Ham   vs   Crystal Palace

Venue : Etihad Stadium

Man City   vs   Fulham

Venue : Goodison Park

Everton   vs   Leicester City

Venue : Elland Road

Leeds United vs Bournemouth

Match Week 16: 12/11/22

Venue : Amex Stadium

Brighton   vs   Aston Villa

Venue : Molineux Stadium

Wolves   vs   Arsenal

Venue : Anfield

Liverpool   vs   Southampton

Venue : Etihad Stadium

Man City   vs   Brentford

Venue : Vitality Stadium

Bournemouth   vs   Everton

Match Week 16: 12/11/22

Venue : St. James' Park

Newcastle   vs   Chelsea

Venue : London Stadium

West Ham   vs   Leicester City

Venue : Tottenham Hotspur Stadium

Tottenham   vs   Leeds United

Venue : Craven Cottage

Fulham   vs   Man United

Venue : The City Ground

Notts Forest   vs   Crystal Palace

Venue: Emirates Stadium

Arsenal   vs   West Ham

Venue : St Mary's Stadium

Southampton   vs   Brighton

Venue : Brentford Community Stadium

Brentford   vs   Tottenham

Venue : Elland Road

Leeds United   vs   Man City

Venue : King Power Stadium

Leicester City vs   Newcastle

Match Week 17: 26/12/22

Venue : Selhurst Park

Crystal Palace   vs   Fulham

Venue : Stamford Bridge

Chelsea   vs   Bournemouth

Venue : Goodison Park

Everton   vs   Wolves

Venue : Old Trafford

Man United   vs   Notts Forest

Venue : Villa Park

Aston Villa   vs   Liverpool

Match Week 18: 31/12/22

Venue : Etihad Stadium

Man City   vs   Everton

Venue : Tottenham Hotspur Stadium

Tottenham   vs   Aston Villa

Venue : Craven Cottage

Fulham   vs   Southampton

Venue : London Stadium

West Ham   vs   Brentford

Venue : Molineux Stadium

Wolves   vs   Man United

 # Match Week 18: 31/12/22

Venue : Vitality Stadium

Bournemouth vs Crystal Palace

Venue : Amex Stadium

Brighton vs Arsenal

Venue : St. James' Park

Newcastle vs Leeds United

Venue : Anfield

Liverpool vs Leicester City

Venue : The City Ground

Notts Forest vs Chelsea

Venue : King Power Stadium

Leicester City   vs   Fulham

Venue : Villa Park

Aston Villa   vs   Wolves

Venue : St Mary's Stadium

Southampton   vs   Notts Forest

Venue : Elland Road

Leeds United   vs   West Ham

Venue: Emirates Stadium

Arsenal   vs   Newcastle

Match Week 19: 2/1/23

Venue : Selhurst Park

Crystal Palace   vs   Tottenham

Venue : Stamford Bridge

Chelsea   vs   Man City

Venue : Brentford Community Stadium

Brentford   vs   Liverpool

Venue : Old Trafford

Man United   vs   Bournemouth

Venue : Goodison Park

Everton   vs   Brighton

Match Week 20: 14/1/23

Venue : Tottenham Hotspur Stadium

Tottenham   vs   Arsenal

Venue : Villa Park

Aston Villa   vs   Leeds United

Venue : Stamford Bridge

Chelsea   vs   Crystal Palace

Venue : Brentford Community Stadium

Brentford   vs   Bournemouth

Venue : Old Trafford

Man United   vs   Man City

Match Week 20: 14/1/23

Venue : Saint Mary's Stadium

Wolves vs **West Ham**

Venue : The City Ground

Notts Forest vs **Leicester City**

Venue : Amex Stadium

Brighton vs **Liverpool**

Venue : St. James' Park

Newcastle vs **Fulham**

Venue : Goodison Park

Everton vs **Southampton**

Match Week 21: 21/1/23

Venue: Emirates Stadium

Arsenal   vs   Man United

Venue : King Power Stadium

Leicester City   vs   Brighton

Venue : St Mary's Stadium

Southampton   vs   Aston Villa

Venue : Craven Cottage

Fulham   vs   Tottenham

Venue : Anfield

Liverpool   vs   Chelsea

Match Week 21: 21/1/23

Venue : Etihad Stadium

Man City   **vs**   **Wolves**

Venue : London Stadium

West Ham   **vs**   **Everton**

Venue : Elland Road

Leeds United   **vs**   **Brentford**

Venue : Selhurst Park

Crystal Palace   **vs**   **Newcastle**

Venue : Vitality Stadium

Bournemouth vs Notts Forest

Match Week 22: 4/2/23

Venue : Amex Stadium

Brighton   vs   Bournemouth

Venue : Old Trafford

Man United   vs   Crystal Palace

Venue : St. James' Park

Newcastle   vs   West Ham

Venue : Brentford Community Stadium

Brentford   vs   Southampton

Venue : Molineux Stadium

Wolves   vs   Liverpool

Venue : Tottenham Hotspur Stadium

Tottenham   vs   Man City

Venue : Villa Park

Aston Villa   vs   Leicester City

Venue : The City Ground

Notts Forest   vs   Leeds United

Venue : Stamford Bridge

Chelsea   vs   Fulham

Venue : Goodison Park

Everton   vs   Arsenal

Match Week 23: 11/2/23

Venue : Etihad Stadium

Man City vs **Aston Villa**

Venue : London Stadium

West Ham vs **Chelsea**

Venue : Craven Cottage

Fulham vs **Notts Forest**

Venue : King Power Stadium

Leicester City vs **Tottenham**

Venue : Vitality Stadium

Bournemouth vs **Newcastle**

Match Week 23: 11/2/23

Venue: Emirates Stadium

Arsenal vs **Brentford**

Venue : Selhurst Park

Crystal Palace vs **Brighton**

Venue : Elland Road

Leeds United vs **Man United**

Venue : St Mary's Stadium

Southampton vs **Wolves**

Venue : Anfield

Liverpool vs **Everton**

Match Week 24: 18/2/23

Venue : Brentford Community Stadium

Brentford   vs   Crystal Palace

Venue : St. James' Park

Newcastle   vs   Liverpool

Venue : Molineux Stadium

Wolves   vs   Bournemouth

Venue : Villa Park

Aston Villa   vs   Arsenal

Venue : Tottenham Hotspur Stadium

Tottenham   vs   West Ham

Match Week 24: 18/2/23

Venue : Amex Stadium

Brighton   vs   Fulham

Venue : Goodison Park

Everton   vs   Leeds United

Venue : Stamford Bridge

Chelsea   vs   Southampton

Venue : Old Trafford

Man United   vs   Leicester City

Venue : The City Ground

Notts Forest   vs   Man City

Match Week 25: 25/2/23

Venue : Goodison Park

Everton   vs   Aston Villa

Venue : Craven Cottage

Fulham   vs   Wolves

Venue : Selhurst Park

Crystal Palace   vs   Liverpool

Venue : King Power Stadium

Leicester City   vs   Arsenal

Venue : London Stadium

West Ham   vs   Notts Forest

Match Week 25: 25/2/23

Venue : St. James' Park

Newcastle   vs   Brighton

Venue : Elland Road

Leeds United   vs   Southampton

Venue : Vitality Stadium

Bournemouth   vs   Man City

Venue : Tottenham Hotspur Stadium

Tottenham   vs   Chelsea

Venue : Old Trafford

Man United   vs   Brentford

Match Week 26: 4/3/23

Venue : Stamford Bridge

Chelsea vs Leeds United

Venue : The City Ground

Notts Forest vs Everton

Venue: Emirates Stadium

Arsenal vs Bournemouth

Venue : Anfield

Liverpool vs Man United

Venue : Villa Park

Aston Villa vs Crystal Palace

Venue : Amex Stadium

Brighton vs West Ham

Venue : St Mary's Stadium

Southampton vs Leicester City

Venue : Etihad Stadium

Man City vs Newcastle

Venue : Molineux Stadium

Wolves vs Tottenham

Venue : Brentford Community Stadium

Brentford vs Fulham

Match Week 27: 11/3/23

Venue : Selhurst Park

Crystal Palace   vs   Man City

Venue : Elland Road

Leeds United   vs   Brighton

Venue : Old Trafford

Man United   vs   Southampton

Venue : Vitality Stadium

Bournemouth vs   Liverpool

Venue : Goodison Park

Everton   vs   Brentford

Match Week 27: 11/3/23

Venue : St. James' Park

Newcastle   vs   Wolves

Venue : London Stadium

West Ham   vs   Aston Villa

Venue : King Power Stadium

Leicester City   vs   Chelsea

Venue : Tottenham Hotspur Stadium

Tottenham   vs   Notts Forest

Venue : Craven Cottage

Fulham   vs   Arsenal

Match Week 28: 18/3/23

Venue: Emirates Stadium

Arsenal   vs   Crystal Palace

Venue : Brentford Community Stadium

Brentford   vs   Leicester City

Venue : The City Ground

Notts Forest   vs   Newcastle

Venue : Anfield

Liverpool   vs   Fulham

Venue : Etihad Stadium

Man City   vs   West Ham

Venue : St Mary's Stadium

Southampton   vs   Tottenham

Venue : Villa Park

Aston Villa   vs   Bournemouth

Venue : Stamford Bridge

Chelsea   vs   Everton

Venue : Amex Stadium

Brighton   vs   Man United

Venue : Molineux Stadium

Wolves   vs   Leeds United

Venue : Vitality Stadium

Bournemouth vs Fulham

Venue : The City Ground

Notts Forest vs Wolves

Venue : Stamford Bridge

Chelsea vs Aston Villa

Venue : Selhurst Park

Crystal Palace vs Leicester City

Venue : St. James' Park

Newcastle vs Man United

Match Week 29: 1/4/23

Venue : London Stadium

West Ham   vs   Southampton

Venue : Etihad Stadium

Man City   vs   Liverpool

Venue: Emirates Stadium

Arsenal   vs   Leeds United

Venue : Amex Stadium

Brighton   vs   Brentford

Venue : Goodison Park

Everton   vs   Tottenham

Match Week 30: 8/4/23

Venue : Villa Park

Aston Villa   vs   Notts Forest

Venue : Brentford Community Stadium

Brentford   vs   Newcastle

Venue : Anfield

Liverpool   vs   Arsenal

Venue : St Mary's Stadium

Southampton   vs   Man City

Venue : Craven Cottage

Fulham   vs   West Ham

Match Week 30: 8/4/23

Venue : Old Trafford

Man United   vs   Everton

Venue : Elland Road

Leeds United   vs   Crystal Palace

Venue : Molineux Stadium

Wolves   vs   Chelsea

Venue : Tottenham Hotspur Stadium

Tottenham   vs   Brighton

Venue : King Power Stadium

Leicester City vs Bournemouth

Match Week 31: 15/4/23

Venue : St Mary's Stadium

Southampton   vs   Crystal Palace

Venue : Goodison Park

Everton   vs   Fulham

Venue : Etihad Stadium

Man City   vs   Leicester City

Venue : Tottenham Hotspur Stadium

Tottenham   vs   Bournemouth

Venue : The City Ground

Notts Forest   vs   Man United

Match Week 31: 15/4/23

Venue : Molineux Stadium

Wolves   vs   Brentford

Venue : Stamford Bridge

Chelsea   vs   Brighton

Venue : London Stadium

West Ham   vs   Arsenal

Venue : Villa Park

Aston Villa   vs   Newcastle

Venue : Elland Road

Leeds United   vs   Liverpool

Match Week 32: 22/4/23

Venue : St. James' Park

Newcastle   vs   Tottenham

Venue : Selhurst Park

Crystal Palace   vs   Everton

Venue : Anfield

Liverpool   vs   Notts Forest

Venue : Vitality Stadium

Bournemouth   vs   West Ham

Venue: Emirates Stadium

Arsenal   vs   Southampton

Match Week 32: 22/4/23

Venue : Amex Stadium

Brighton   **vs**   **Man City**

Venue : Brentford Community Stadium

Brentford   **vs**   **Aston Villa**

Venue : King Power Stadium

Leicester City   **vs**   **Wolves**

Venue : Craven Cottage

Fulham   **vs**   **Leeds United**

Venue : Old Trafford

Man United   **vs**   **Chelsea**

Match Week 33: 25/4/23

Venue : Tottenham Hotspur Stadium

Tottenham   vs   Man United

Venue : Elland Road

Leeds United   vs   Leicester City

Venue : The City Ground

Notts Forest   vs   Brighton

Venue : London Stadium

West Ham   vs   Liverpool

Venue : Molineux Stadium

Wolves   vs   Crystal Palace

Match Week 33: 25/4/23

Venue : Goodison Park

Everton   **vs**   **Newcastle**

Venue : Villa Park

Aston Villa   **vs**   **Fulham**

Venue : St Mary's Stadium

Southampton   **vs**   **Bournemouth**

Venue : Stamford Bridge

Chelsea   **vs**   **Brentford**

Venue : Etihad Stadium

Man City   **vs**   **Arsenal**

Match Week 34: 29/4/23

Venue : Old Trafford

Man United   vs   **Aston Villa**

Venue : Amex Stadium

Brighton   vs   **Wolves**

Venue : Craven Cottage

Fulham   vs   **Man City**

Venue : Brentford Community Stadium

Brentford   vs   **Notts Forest**

Venue : King Power Stadium

Leicester City   vs   **Everton**

Venue: Emirates Stadium

Arsenal   vs   Chelsea

Venue : Vitality Stadium

Bournemouth vs   Leeds United

Venue : Anfield

Liverpool   vs   Tottenham

Venue : Selhurst Park

Crystal Palace vs   West Ham

Venue : St. James' Park

Newcastle   vs   Southampton

Match Week 35: 6/5/23

Venue : London Stadium

West Ham   vs   Man United

Venue : Vitality Stadium

Bournemouth   vs   Chelsea

Venue : Etihad Stadium

Man City   vs   Leeds United

Venue : The City Ground

Notts Forest   vs   Southampton

Venue : St. James' Park

Newcastle   vs   Arsenal

Match Week 35: 6/5/23

Venue : Craven Cottage

Fulham   vs   Leicester City

Venue : Anfield

Liverpool   vs   Brentford

Venue : Amex Stadium

Brighton   vs   Everton

Venue : Molineux Stadium

Wolves   vs   Aston Villa

Venue : Tottenham Hotspur Stadium

Tottenham   vs   Crystal Palace

Match Week 36: 13/5/23

Venue : Goodison Park

Everton vs **Man City**

Venue : St Mary's Stadium

Southampton vs **Fulham**

Venue : Brentford Community Stadium

Brentford vs **West Ham**

Venue: Emirates Stadium

Arsenal vs **Brighton**

Venue : Stamford Bridge

Chelsea vs **Notts Forest**

Match Week 36: 13/5/23

Venue : King Power Stadium

Leicester City   vs   Liverpool

Venue : Villa Park

Aston Villa   vs   Tottenham

Venue : Old Trafford

Man United   vs   Wolves

Venue : Selhurst Park

Crystal Palace   vs   Bournemouth

Venue : Elland Road

Leeds United   vs   Newcastle

Match Week 37: 20/5/23

Venue : London Stadium

West Ham vs **Leeds United**

Venue : Anfield

Liverpool vs **Aston Villa**

Venue : Amex Stadium

Brighton vs **Southampton**

Venue : Tottenham Hotspur Stadium

Tottenham vs **Brentford**

Venue : Molineux Stadium

Wolves vs **Everton**

Match Week 37: 20/5/23

Venue : The City Ground

Notts Forest   vs   Arsenal

Venue : St. James' Park

Newcastle   vs   Leicester City

Venue : Vitality Stadium

Bournemouth   vs   Man United

Venue : Etihad Stadium

Man City   vs   Chelsea

Venue : Craven Cottage

Fulham   vs   Crystal Palace

Match Week 38: 28/5/23

Venue : Villa Park

Aston Villa   vs   Brighton

Venue : Goodison Park

Everton   vs   Bournemouth

Venue : Elland Road

Leeds United   vs   Tottenham

Venue : Brentford Community Stadium

Brentford   vs   Man City

Venue : Old Trafford

Man United   vs   Fulham

Match Week 38: 28/5/23

Venue : Stamford Bridge

Chelsea   vs   Newcastle

Venue : King Power Stadium

Leicester City   vs   West Ham

Venue: Emirates Stadium

Arsenal   vs   Wolves

Venue : St Mary's Stadium

Southampton vs   Liverpool

Venue : Selhurst Park

Crystal Palace vs   Notts Forest

Scan The QR Code To Check Out More Utopia Press Books On Amazon!

  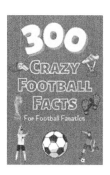

Printed in Great Britain
by Amazon

82395981R00045